META MORPHOSIS

Wet Sidewalks II

by TOM TYPINSKI

DEDICATION

To The News and the brews and the bros and those who shared time on the line watching paper while I got to write poetry.

CONTENTS

WET SIDEWALKS	4
JURY DUTY	4
TUMBLE	5
MISS MIST	5
COLLINS SUNRISE	6
WORDS TO NEWCOMERS	7
DO YOU KNOW HIM?	8
DATE	9
THE COLOR OF THIS PLACE	9
AUTUMN	10
BUTTERFLY	10
LIBERATING SPRING	11
RUN	12
AN END (TO DANNY)	13
THANK GOD FOR THIS LITTLE BIT OF SILENCE	14
BLEW LIGHT	14
FLIGHT	15
SPLITTING SECONDS	16
VOODOO DOLL LOVE	17
FIELDS OF ICE	18
KUNDERA SUNSET	19
AMBIVALENCE	20
HOW GOOD TO KNOW WHERE TALENT LAYS	21
DIGITAL DREAMS	22

<u>WET SIDEWALKS</u>

When you walk
the street in the rain;
the rhythm that
the puddles make,
the plunking sounds
that only water can mumble;
the song that hearts sing hardest
when they cannot be heard
make you feel cemented and
disconnected, like rain in wind

The feet carry their weight across
islands of dry pavement
steps stole from potholes
to shadows to blackness
and back.
Not quite dry but
waterless enough to keep
shoes drier,
the mind clear, the eyes unblinking.

A movie (you are thankful for the time)
a memory (you are grateful for what is shared)
a day spent lonely (you are searching for what is there)
to test how the soul's developed (or hasn't)

You curse yourself and her and restaurant food.
You douse yourself with another beer.
You resent the rain and wind and your youth
for fooling you to believe you are the same
as everyone.

<u>JURY DUTY</u>

So formal, technical etiquette
as the understanding lay,
sit sleepily in their seats.
Nodding not in recognition
but in shaking themselves awake.
Forced attention by duty to the
Government System.

They are, one and all, paid to be bored,
paid very little,
barely minimum wage.
Rage reigns in their eyes with each
stupid inquiry.
Incessant questioning, pro/con
to win the purse.
For it all comes to money
whatever injury occurred
be it mental or physical or spiritual
it can all be counted and gauged in dollars.

Justice for Dollars!
As they take turns spinning wheels
going nowhere, the roulette ball falls;
but here, tomorrow.
They'll return.
And a judgement without thought
but more money spent in rendering
a conclusion will be bought.

<u>TUMBLE</u>

Images like chips falling,
being collected by Medusa's superglue
forming a mosaic of varying tiles
spelling "life" in the language of symbols.

The language universal in content
yet, symbolistically
different, per culture;
"Your Devil is My God" mentality
when one says what he sees

Interpretation only one key to
the myriad tumblers holding the
combination of beliefs
each deductible to Me

<u>MISS MIST</u>

In the midst of a morning walk
I saw you clearly
dancing with who might have been
had the angels other intentions
Scenes from our talks
waltzed with the sun
spun hope in webs of rope
wet with dew.
I thought more of you.

COLLINS SUNRISE

Every day the sunrise is different
Round as an orange juice stain;
yet ever day it is there, here,
where it never rains.

It greets you openly
and will come
whether you show up or not.

The birds get fed,
the people move
forth and back on the boardwalk
for only to keep moving;
or stop, collecting its magnificence
on face and exposed skin.

Each day there, like the waves,
sometimes swirling, sometimes placid,
sometimes crashing so loud you can't hear the gulls;
but always there, silent as God,

Joining in the ascent
from slumber to brightness
to new light.

It feeds me as much as food;
the way people greet each other,
the way they walk or run,
just to watch the sun rise up from the sea;
so undeniably present
doing the one thing it's meant to do best
rise;
giving joy without trying
giving by being, itself, free.

<u>WORD TO NEWCOMERS</u>

Only the hypocrites
Need to apply
Two faces minimum
Know how to lie
Tell and trust no one
Knives twist in your back
No one believes when
You tell them the facts
Friends aren't true
They'll turn at first chance
Make you look bad
Then deny their stance
Don't try to be brave
Or fight for what's right
They'll humble you up
Or shoot you on sight
The biggest group of cowards
You'll ever imagine
Hang together here
In gang-fight fashion
They bunch up and holler
At every mistake
Never admit wrongness
Never give a break
So beware these morons
These peons called peers.
Just believe in yourself
And you've nothing to fear.

<u>DO YOU KNOW HIM?</u>

You're down in a hole
and you reach for a goal
soon prayer and work helps you find it.

Arrangements are made
but there's bills to be paid
You see things only in tid-bits.

Things start going fine
you're drunk in your wine
But along the way tend to forget

That being at the top
or even reaching for it
causes heartache one rung
from worthless bullshit.

You've spread yourself thin
now the water you're in
is so deep you wish you'd had fins.

All the friends who were close
see only your pose
as you pointedly wallow in sin.

You've got all you want
but you should have sought need
once again you're alone in the pit.

When seeking success
you must not forget
the One who helped most,
know Him.

DATE

fun
no fun
she loves him
she loves him not
he wants to get to it
she just wants it done
she in the tubetop and cigarette skirt
he in the imitation Hemingway brushjacket
yawning to keep cognizance
the wine adding to the blurr
knees nudging at a table for two
hardly big enough for one
the server checking out her
he checking out the server
she checking out the door
she loves him not
she loathes him
no fun
done

THE COLOR OF THIS PLACE

Grays and Blues, faces askew
The color of this place by day
Nighttime comes, still the same
No windows to tell it's changed.
Papers strewn like a gerbil' s cage.
The daily dust rearranged.
Amongst the rubble – the faces,
stubbled masks of brighter days.
The Color of This Place.

<u>AUTUMN</u>

Come, calm your stomach
I'll hold you until dawn
Autumn's falling.
We'll watch leaves leaving branches
or butterflies dance;
those quick cool evenings
to walk in alluring romance.

Sing "Chelsea Morning"
of waffles and jam
a time of good loving
no "I don't or I cant's"
in cable-knit sweaters, and corduroy pants.
When we'll both gamble, but not take a chance.
Both proving our real love, both taking a stance.

<u>BUTTERFLY</u>

A living picture of symmetry
A painting set to motion
starch white, barely there
teasing at vain grasps
not taking any chances
dancing on air
to the whirr of bare branches

No longer crawling
but grown to full beauty
legs lost, fur fallen
with wings of powdered translucence.
She lands lightly
to ice the already glowing rose
then soon disenchanted
she leaves as she landed.

LIBERATING SPRING

Cyclic channels circle 360
the difference being clothing and skin
as the first warm breeze
squeezes through screens
and the box opens
for Pandora's pupils
reclaiming freedom in
the liberating spring

Beginning at the end
of winter's freeze
like messengers of clear intent
sent to reveal treasures left
in dewed mornings
glistening iridescently to sunset
harmoniously pulsing to the
symphony of sparrows
and the solo coo of the dove
showing off

HIGH LIGHTS
Rock & Roll never dies
it just changes its hair color.

PRISMFISH
Diving deep down
I circled the coral reef
and watched, as prisms of rainbow fish
dashed quickly in directions
reflexively from my reach

<u>RUN</u>

Reaching the crest of the hill breathless
Marietta stretched to patterned pastures
and horse fences zig zagging perimeters
of openness like paper towels blot liquid
borderless, unlimited, marked with dots of dwellings
set off like parenthesed sentences
inside stories that mattered only to those living them.

The wind weighed of apple blossoms and hyacinths
the music of the moment bore breath, crickets, silence
the murmuring of birds chirping in their quest for breakfast.

The colors so dark - green, blue, white - vast, majestic;
only possibly captured in pupils of the artist with
the wisdom to know he can't;
land and elements rising naturally,
like fog finding focus
in the obscurity of daylight.

Through
a green
brown
flowering
moist
silent
forest
I spot
a fawn;
Bambi
I presume.

<u>AN END (to Danny)</u>

Once
and lastly
He came to bid adieu
to close the circle of friendship
neither of us knew

He, in quest of something
anciently new
and I, into cocoon of family

We threw our hats and scarves toward
the slick-beat of sleet
shook hands and wished for better
love, luck, truth, virtue

and understood the task
was not to touch another
with words or prose

but to find what pleased our minds
our eyes, our souls -
something only alluded to -
Our Youth.

<u>THANK GOD FOR THIS LITTLE BIT OF SILENCE</u>

The machines of "me" are humming
making everything oblivious
though the fan whirrs
and the record purrs,
not much registers
except words.

Everything is looking at me
inanimate faces from snapshots
and carvings of rough crystal, ivory and pewter;
even Marilyn stares in her drunken stupor, curbed,
like so many of my heroes
who've lived in the blurr.
Drunken heroes, men of words
H.M., E.H., P.T., J.K., T.T.

<u>BLEW LIGHT</u>

Waxing poetic in the blue light of TV
beyond the eve of belief
musical acquaintances of the late night type
when spirits walk and angels sleep
dreamless revered friends,
ones I keep beneath
my pillow next to crystals which protect
or take me deep,
deeper than the surface
of wakefulness or deceit.
Each moment's consciousness
felt like breath on the nape,
someone over me, 3-D in relief.
Watchful. Careful. Philosophical. Beginning Being.

<u>FLIGHT</u>

In all my seriousness
I was too tense
to be glib
to give a pat answer
to what she knew I knew.

So she lay me back
holding my wrists
while kissing my stomach
as I winced wondering
what was working
and what wasn't;
A chemical imbalance of emotions.

In this flight of fantasy
I flew on a suspended thread
above my bed like Charlotte.
A charlatan to the actual
projected but not present.
The eagerness in which
I wished it to happen dissipated
like the shudder emotions left on

Completely detached we sat up, sidled
let the vibrations of heat and honesty
tingle between elbows and knees
entwined our thoughts
a pool surrounding
flesh peninsulas
We spoke. We kissed.
We wished each other sweet dreams
with lucid dips
wondering in the dark
where the lives we'd dreamed
had been misplaced.

<u>SPLITTING SECONDS (THE BEAUTY IN BLUE)</u>

One day
when dressed in model-best
a certain light caught your eyes
impossible to describe
but someone else caught
the reflection in a lens
as there you sat
fringed, coiffed,
earrings dangling
looking back
perched coy on the ottoman
dress straps dropped
and for a second
all planets stopped
and magic happened
to salute this presence of you
The Beauty In Blue.

COFFEE

Black coffee and
black toast
Won't see me do
either one of those

The coffee makes me gag
and the toast makes me choke
so orange juice and bagels
extra pulp, heavy salt
two.

<u>VOODOO DOLL LOVE</u>   <u>1986</u>

so you wait
you waited
feeling glum
until the numbness
overtakes your face

The tears
frozen crystals
too often spent
trickle trenches
to your chin
you've given in
again

Feeling friendless
misled
no direction and
you're fed up
with love's pins

voodoo doll loving can't win

<u>*MATHEMATICAL LOGIC*</u>
Life equals Love squared

<u>FIELDS OF ICE</u>

Only with a winter rain
can you witness God's polyurethane
The seal so hard and clear it
can only be melted by breath and tears
fields like lakes to the left and right
where road workers construct roads
from their destruction of dirt and ice
lights in amber patterns telling, steering
cars left and right and what begins the
morning is what was left of the night.

The guard in his wax museum station
asleep like a dead gray man in an
upright casket; eyes closed, head erect
as he slumbers dreaming of warmth and home
and not the bone chilling bite of the
wind of his 3-paned sight.

Somber as a sleeping cat I crunch through
the lot gingerly slipping, wishing I'd
had my skates and my youth so I could
put the ice to use with time minus hands

A man salutes my entry with a wave as
I say to myself some lines from a poem
which I'm composing as I parade to the stairs
leading me away from this day to dreariness and pay -
and that four letter word called W O R K.

<u>KUNDERA SUNSET</u>

The beauty of a sunset
words by Kundera
so passionate, so warm
overwhelming my senses
showering my shoulders
with the lightness of depth
sanctifying my belief
in myself and in man
standing waist deep in
cleansing sea, breathing
the mists of ion-charged air,
ratifying belief
that all is here, is there
in a heart, in a teardrop
in a sigh and a smile
cascading in jettisons
like liquid blessings
where the soul flies
uninhibited on wings
of freedom, being
nothing but itself
without qualm or
reason, a desire
only to see clearly
to the beginnings
of nature, when
man and creature
share food and dwelling
side by side, unbridled
by commands, blows
or reprimands.

<u>AMBIVALENCE</u>

The yin vs. yang school of
deliverance
To come clean or keep
polluting with caffeine
and fat and HDL
The diet swings like a baseball
bat's whack
There you are back on the
same train again
Derailed without details
floating in the yards of
despair
You no longer dare
You don't care
And all the creeps awake in
your dreams seep into
your waking
Taking your hopes and
replacing with fears
your daylight musings
because too often they
haven't come true.

But it's up to you.
to
Drop the past
like something thrown aside
Delusions about what had
or hadn't been done

Step up from the back
of century's cycle "numero uno"
Resplendent and Indifferent
equal goals to fears

"Rise above"
"It's not so bad"
More Knowledge for every Tear.

HOW GOOD TO KNOW WHERE TALENT LAYS

When pen sets to writing
It takes direction from something
set in the mind, celestial
something God given
much more than pen vs. page

When brilliance lights
and remains
more than seconds
when the chance to turn in
begins transformations
from thoughts to ideas to images
to scenes to dreams to visions
so complete
it's as if footprints lay
painted like
Arthur Murray
dance steps

Where you waltz through
feelings with ease and
contentment because
they're your own original
unabashed invention
sense made from senses
desires derived from drives
of passion

Advancing to higher stages
of wisdom in the
dandelions of chance
spun whirly-bird like
on the wind of change

Cartwheels on a playground
back-flips on trampolines
The tossed salad that is life
delivered with the ease of speech.

<u>DIGITAL DREAMS</u>

All points
A to Z
are weaved
with seams of transition

Axis points
set coordinates
on where to turn
or to traverse

Each chemically
genetically connected

Archetypes to Icons
Symbols to synapses
Images come redundant to
the doormat of Inner Self

All have keys
gaining interest by
preordained chances
forming matrixes for recollection
reiterated clues of childhood dances
Askew views for sacrosanct looting
memories booted, all this and therapy too!

META MORPHOSIS